LET'S LEARN ABOUT SPACE

THE SOLAR SYSTEM

Rebecca Kraft Rector

Enslow Publishing
101 W. 23rd Street
Suite 240
New York, NY 10011
USA
enslow.com

Words to Know

asteroid A chunk of rock in outer space that orbits the sun.

comet A chunk of ice, gas, and dust in outer space that orbits the sun.

galaxy A large group of stars, clouds of gas, and dust.

gravity The force that attracts two bodies to each other.

orbit The path of an object as it circles another object in space.

CONTENTS

WORDS TO KNOW 2

WHAT IS A SOLAR SYSTEM? 5

OUR PLACE IN SPACE 7

FORMING A SOLAR SYSTEM 9

THE SUN 11

THE PLANETS 13

REMEMBER THE ORDER 15

ASTEROIDS AND COMETS 17

BEYOND THE PLANETS 19

THE EDGE OF
THE SOLAR SYSTEM 21

ACTIVITY: MAKE A SPACE HAT 22

LEARN MORE 24

INDEX 24

The solar system includes the sun, planets, the moon, asteroids, and comets.

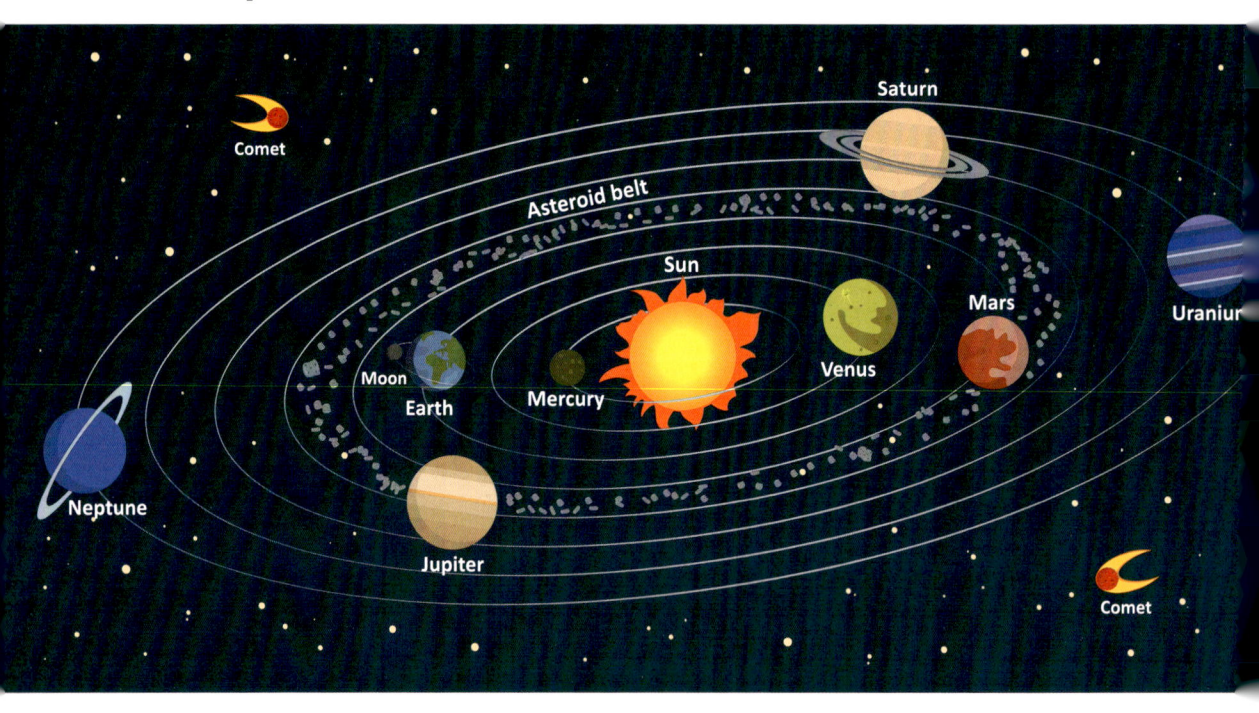

What Is a Solar System?

A solar system is a sun and everything that orbits it. It has planets and moons. It has asteroids and comets.

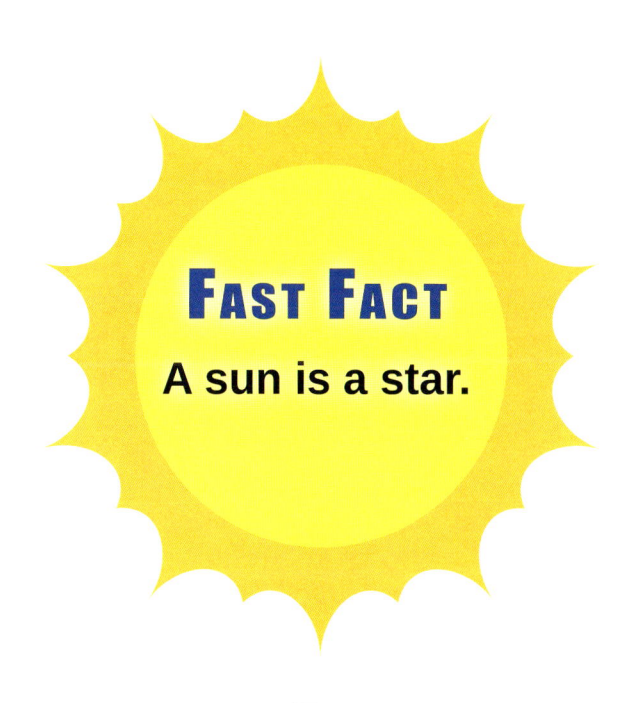

Fast Fact

A sun is a star.

Our solar system is just one small part of our galaxy, the Milky Way.

Our Place in Space

Our solar system is in a **galaxy**. The galaxy is called the Milky Way. The solar system orbits the galaxy. It takes 225 million years for one orbit.

Fast Fact
Billions of solar systems are in the Milky Way.

These pictures show how the solar system formed when a cloud of gas and dust collapsed.

Forming a Solar System

The solar system formed from a cloud of gas. Gravity pulled the cloud into pieces. The largest piece became the sun. Others became planets. Smaller pieces became asteroids and comets.

Fast Fact

The solar system is 4.5 billion years old.

The planets orbit around the sun.

The Sun

Our solar system has one sun. The sun is the center of the solar system. It is the largest object. Other objects orbit around it.

Fast Fact

Most of the solar system is empty space.

There are four inner planets and four outer planets.

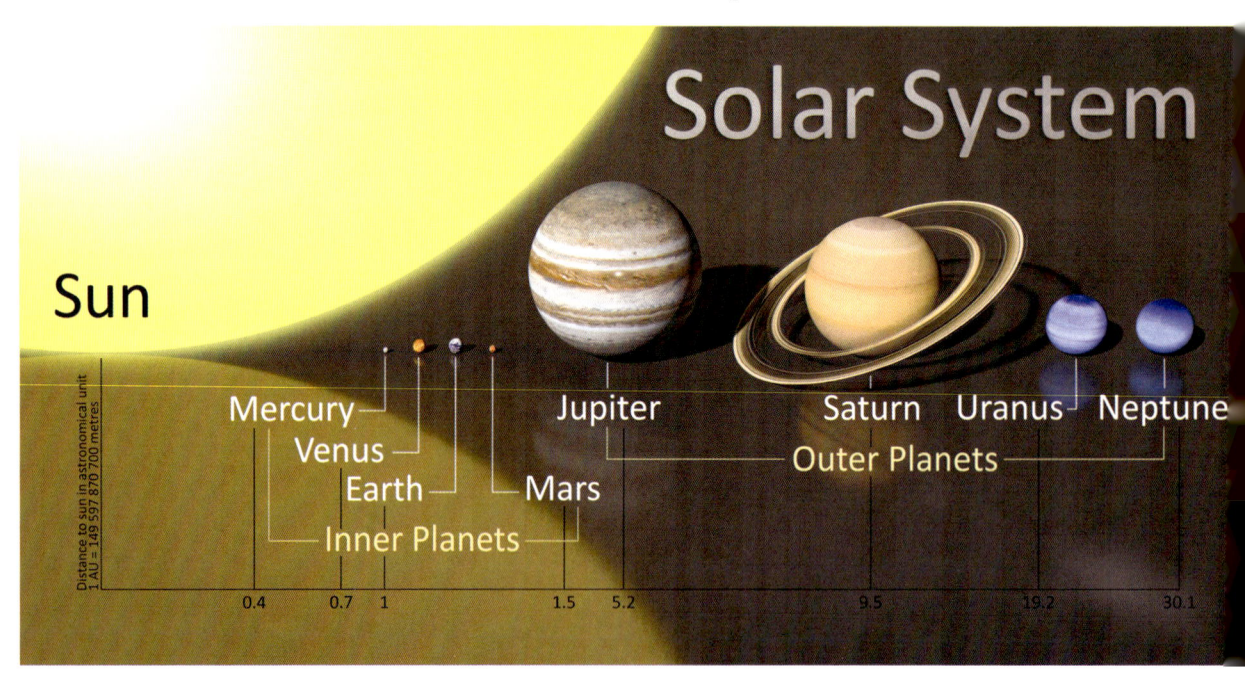

Solar System

Sun

Distance to sun in astronomical unit
1 AU = 149 597 870 700 metres

Mercury — 0.4
Venus — 0.7
Earth — 1
Mars — 1.5
Inner Planets

Jupiter — 5.2
Saturn — 9.5
Uranus — 19.2
Neptune — 30.1
Outer Planets

The Planets

Four planets are called inner planets. They are closest to the sun. They are Mercury, Venus, Earth, and Mars. The four outer planets are Jupiter, Saturn, Uranus, and Neptune.

Fast Fact

The outer planets are bigger than the inner planets.

You can use the first letter of the planets to remember their order.

Remember the Order

Here is a way to remember the order of the planets. Use the first letters of these words: **M**y **V**ery **E**ducated **M**other **J**ust **S**erved **U**s **N**achos.

Fast Fact

Neptune is the farthest planet from the sun.

A comet streaks across the sky.

Asteroids and Comets

Asteroids and comets also orbit the sun. Asteroids are chunks of rock. Comets are chunks of ice. They were left over when the planets formed.

The Kuiper Belt is mostly made up of icy objects. Some are very small, and others are many miles wide.

Beyond the Planets

The Kuiper Belt lies beyond the planets. It is a ring of icy bodies. Pluto is in this ring. Pluto used to be called a planet. Now it is called a dwarf planet.

In this picture, the sun is in the center. The Oort Cloud is the outer shell, far from the sun and the planets.

The Edge of the Solar System

The Oort Cloud is at the solar system's edge. It contains icy pieces. The pieces can be as big as mountains. The cloud surrounds the solar system.

Fast Fact

Comets come from the Kuiper Belt and the Oort Cloud.

Activity

Make a Space Hat

MATERIALS

Black construction paper
White paper
Scissors
Glue
Crayons

You can wear the solar system! Let's get started!

Procedure:

Step 1: Cut the construction paper in half lengthwise.

Step 2: Glue the pieces into one band about two feet long.

Step 3: Make circles on the white paper. You need eight planets and a sun.

Step 4: Cut them out and color them.

Step 5: Glue them onto the long band.

Step 6: Label the planets. Be sure they're in order.

Step 7: Glue the band into a loop that fits your head.

Now the solar system is on your head!

Solar System

Be the center of your own solar system!

Planets

LEARN MORE

Books

DK. *DK Find Out! Solar System*. New York, NY: DK, 2016.

It's All About...Super Solar System. New York, NY: Kingfisher, 2016.

Sparrow, Giles. *Our Solar System*. New York, NY: Enslow, 2018.

Websites

Kids Know It Network
kidsastronomy.com/astronomy-games/make-a-solar-system
Add planets, comets, and asteroids to build a solar system in this fun game.

NASA: The Solar System
starchild.gsfc.nasa.gov/docs/StarChild/solar_system_level1/solar_system.html
Discover fun facts about the solar system.

INDEX

asteroids, 5, 9, 17
comets, 5, 9, 17
formation, 9
galaxy, 7
gravity, 9
Kuiper Belt, 19, 21
Milky Way, 7
moon, 5
Oort Cloud, 21
orbit, 7, 11
planets, 5, 9, 13, 15, 17, 19
Pluto, 19
sun, 5, 9, 11, 13, 15, 17

Published in 2020 by Enslow Publishing, LLC.
101 W. 23rd Street, Suite 240, New York, NY 10011

Copyright © 2020 by Enslow Publishing, LLC.

All rights reserved.

No part of this book may be reproduced by any means without the written permission of the publisher.

Library of Congress Cataloging-in-Publication Data

Names: Rector, Rebecca Kraft, author.
Title: The solar system / Rebecca Kraft Rector.
Description: New York : Enslow Publishing, 2020. | Series: Let's learn about space | Audience: Grade K to 4. | Includes bibliographical references and index.
Identifiers: LCCN 2018041874| ISBN 9781978507319 (library bound) | ISBN 9781978509337 (pbk.) | ISBN 9781978509344 (6 pack)
Subjects: LCSH: Solar system—Juvenile literature. | Planets—Juvenile literature. Classification: LCC QB501.3 .R44 2019 | DDC 523.4—dc23
LC record available at https://lccn.loc.gov/2018041874

Printed in the United States of America

To Our Readers: We have done our best to make sure all website addresses in this book were active and appropriate when we went to press. However, the author and the publisher have no control over and assume no liability for the material available on those websites or on any websites they may link to. Any comments or suggestions can be sent by e-mail to customerservice@enslow.com.

Photos Credits: Cover, p. 1 adventtr/E+/Getty Images; p. 4 Chulkova Nina/Shutterstock.com; p. 6 Mark Garlick/Science Source; p. 8 Milena Moiola/Shutterstock.com; p. 10 shooarts/Shutterstock.com; p. 12 Markus Gann/Shutterstock.com; p. 14 Macrovector/Shutterstock.com; p. 16 Universal Images Group/Getty Images; p. 18 Paul Fleet/500Px Plus/Getty Images; p. 20 Spencer Sutton/Science Source; p. 23 TashaNatasha/Shutterstock.com; interior design elements (planets) Vectomart/Shutterstock.com, (sun) Kirill Kirsanov/Shutterstock.com.